ideals®
EASTER

D1384959

JANUARY 2003

Dedicated to a celebration—through poetry and prose—of the American ideals of faith in God, loyalty to country, and love of family.

The flowers appear on the earth; the time of the singing of birds is come.
—*Song of Solomon 2:12a*

IDEALS—Vol. 60, No. 1 January 2003 IDEALS (ISSN 0019-137X, USPS 256-240) is published six times a year: January, March, May, July, September, and November by IDEALS PUBLICATIONS, a division of Guideposts, 39 Seminary Hill Road, Carmel, NY 10512. Copyright © 2003 by IDEALS PUBLICATIONS, a division of Guideposts. All rights reserved. The cover and entire contents of IDEALS are fully protected by copyright and must not be reproduced in any manner whatsoever. Title IDEALS registered U.S. Patent Office. Printed and bound in USA by Quebecor Printing. Printed on Weyerhaeuser Husky. The paper used in this publication meets the minimum requirements of American National Standard for Information Sciences—Permanence of Paper for Printed Library Materials, ANSI Z39.48-1984. Periodicals postage paid at Carmel, New York, and additional mailing offices. POSTMASTER: Send address changes to Ideals, 39 Seminary Hill Road, Carmel, NY 10512. For subscription or customer service questions, contact Ideals Publications, a division of Guideposts, 39 Seminary Hill Road, Carmel, NY 10512. Fax 845-228-2115. Reader Preference Service: We occasionally make our mailing lists available to other companies whose products or services might interest you. If you prefer not to be included, please write to Ideals Customer Service.

ISBN 0-8249-1205-5 GST 893989236

Visit the *Ideals* website at www.idealsbooks.com

Cover photo: Cherry tree, Hartford, Connecticut. Photo by William H. Johnson.
Inside Front Cover: TOPIARY TEA. Sherri Buck Baldwin, artist. Copyright © 2003 by Sherri Buck Baldwin. Courtesy of Main Street Press Limited.
Inside Back Cover: VASE OF FLOWERS. Claude Monet, artist. Image from Superstock.

In This Issue

Young Spring
Ruth B. Field

The springtime weaves a silver spell
Of things more sweet than words can tell—
The echoes of sweet music sung,
The burnished dreams, forever young,
Of every spring since dawn of time—
And every heartbeat knows its rhyme.
The flowering earth, the rapturous wings,
And all the joy of springtime sings
As youth goes down its blossomed ways
And hand in hand with beauty strays.
From winter's drab cocoonlike light,
The silken butterflies take flight,
And young love lingers in their gleams
To gather all their rainbow dreams.

An Offering
Emma S. McLaughlin

I wish my hands could gather
Into one bright bouquet
The miracle of April
That fills this Sabbath day:

Forsythia, shafts of sunlight,
Chalice of daffodils,
The morning hymn of bird song
That lifts from greening hills,

The caroling of church bells,
Rare essence of perfume
Ascending from camellias
All starry-eyed with bloom.

Then I would come so humbly
And offer it to you,
Wrapped in the tissue of the fog,
Sweet with the wine of dew.

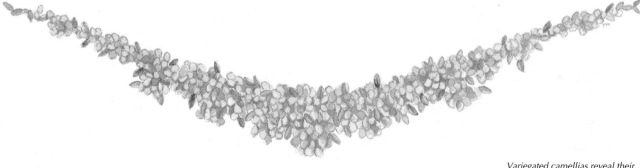

*Variegated camellias reveal their
spectacular petals in Multnomah County,
Oregon. Photo by Steve Terrill.*

When Early March

James Whitcomb Riley

When country roads begin to thaw
In mottled spots of damp and dust,
And fences by the margin draw
Along the frosty crust
Their graphic silhouettes, I say,
The spring is coming round this way.

When morning-time is bright with sun
And keen with wind, and both confuse
The dancing, glancing eyes of one
With tears that ooze and ooze,
And nose-tips weep as well as they,
The spring is coming round this way.

When suddenly some shadow-bird
Goes wavering beneath the gaze;
And through the hedge the moan is heard
Of kine that fain would graze
In grasses new, I smile and say,
The spring is coming round this way.

When knotted horsetails are untied
And teamsters whistle here and there,
And clumsy mitts are laid aside
And choppers' hands are bare,
And chips are thick where children play,
The spring is coming round this way.

When through the twigs the farmer tramps,
And troughs are chunked beneath the trees,
And fragrant hints of sugar-camps
Astray in every breeze;
When early March seems middle May,
The spring is coming round this way.

When coughs are changed to laughs, and when
Our frowns melt into smiles of glee,
And all our blood thaws out again
In streams of ecstasy,
And poets wreak their roundelay,
The spring is coming round this way.

*A chartreuse ground cover brightens a walnut orchard that waits
for spring near Colusa, California. Photo by Dennis Frates.*

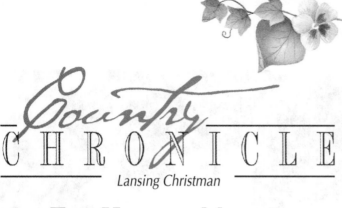

Country CHRONICLE

Lansing Christman

The Hope of March

The March snowmelt—what joy is in that day when the morning sun starts spreading its warming rays over a land under snow, penetrating the crusted banks along the south side of stone walls and hedges. What joy I find to watch the water drip from the weathered eaves of roofs of houses and barns facing south.

The sap will rise today, and I will think back to my early years on the farm when I would tap the roadside maples near the house. I may think of those spring days of splitting firewood by the woodhouse not far from the kitchen door.

I know the creek will open from the thaw, and I will hear the loud splashing song of the Bozenkill that winds by the house where I was born. I will see and hear the rushing, thumping masses of ice sweeping downstream with the current.

During this month of the vernal equinox, the hours of sunlight equal those of darkness; and the days will grow longer until the summer solstice in June.

March is a month of hope, of looking ahead, of closing the doors to winter and opening them to another spring. Snows may yet sweep down upon the land, but each day of longer sun brightens my pathway through the hours of an ebbing wintertime.

The author of three books, Lansing Christman has contributed to Ideals for almost thirty years. Mr. Christman has also been published in several American, international, and braille anthologies. He lives in rural South Carolina.

Yellow pansies are determined to find the sun in Corvallis, Oregon. Photo by Dennis Frates.

Pure and perfect, sweet arbutus twines her rosy-tinted wreath.

Arbutus

Evelyn Gates Shisler

The first and fairest to appear
Beneath our northern tasseled pine
Is the sweet, modest, fairy bloom
Of the lowly arbutus vine.
No other blossom is so rare
Or has a fragrance so divine
Or is so honored and so prized
In any other land or clime.

Dear fairy bloom, thou art to me
So pure, so modest, and so sweet—
A symbol of true innocence
With which all life should be replete.
Young love should be as pure as thee,
As brave and unafraid to live,
As clean, as perfect, and as true—
The fairest gift that life can give.

*Above and opposite: White and pink arbutus blossoms dot
the woodland floor. Photos by John Heidecker.*

Hail the flower whose early bridal makes the festival of spring!—Elaine Goodale

Pink Pledge

Frank Dempster Sherman

Along the woods' brown edge
The Wind goes wandering
To find the first pink pledge,
The hint of spring.

The withered leaves around,
She scatters every one
And gives to wintry ground
A glimpse of sun.

And to the woodland, dumb
And desolate so long,
She calls the birds to come
With happy song.

Then the arbutus! This
The pledge, the hint she sought,
The blush, the breath, the kiss,
Spring's very thought!

*Overleaf: Delphiniums, foxgloves, and daisies fill a garden created inside a
demolished barn's foundation in Cassopolis, Michigan. Photo by Jessie Walker.*

The First Tulip

Lucille Veneklasen

Alone among the garden's green—
A single bit of red;
In quiet majesty it stands
And nods its pretty head.
Soon others will be blooming,
Their brilliant beauty seen;
But none more lovely than the first
Among the garden's green.

Red tulips paint a flower bed in the Netherlands. Photo by Superstock.

Moment of Wonder

Sarah Lynn Phillips

A bit of bulb
dropped unnoticed
from my hand
late last fall
yields one tiny
blossomed jewel,
cradled
in the hand
of a squatting child
on a sunny day.

VINTAGE EASTER TOYS

Laurie Hunter

When my two children celebrated their first Easters, I took great care to select a special stuffed bunny for each of them. My daughter's was a floppy bunny handmade from old quilts. My son's was a vintage jointed rabbit who wore a drum around his neck. I had grand visions of these special bunnies beginning a new tradition and waiting for the children on Easter Sunday each year. So it was truly traumatic when I knocked over my mug of coffee just before the children awoke one Easter morning a couple of years later, causing both bunnies to be soaked up to their cottontails.

Resolving to replace the hares with equally unique and lovable Easter bunnies, I placed a small ad in our community newspaper that asked for "interesting" antique Easter bunnies. Within a few days, I received a helpful letter describing a pair of Easter bunnies who came with "accessories numbering fifty-eight to be precise." With my curiosity sufficiently piqued and my hopes high, I called the respondent and set up an appointment.

Because the seller could see I would provide a loving home for her treasures, she bequeathed her collection to me on the spot. Our family's new celebrated "Mr. and Mrs. Easter Bunny Extraordinaire" were propped up inside an old suitcase brimming with Easter trinkets: several dress-up outfits for the honored hares, a pair of chick-shaped china egg holders, antique golden Easter eggs, a wooden jigsaw puzzle depicting a Victorian Easter egg hunt, a miniature rocking-horse rabbit, tin candy holders, diminutive cotton bunnies, and so much more. The rabbits themselves were the crowning centerpiece. Both early Steiff rabbits from the 1940s, one bunny fashioned in realistic mohair stood on his hind paws and wore a snappy taffeta collar. The other bunny was an albino woolen rabbit with worn white fur and red eyes. This stunning beginning to my collection sparked an entirely new hobby: collecting vintage Easter toys of all kinds.

My collection now includes a number of rare Easter toys and a few one-of-a-kind treasures. One prize find is a vintage hen basket dating back to about 1910. Made in Germany, it sports a paper hen resting atop a cardboard nest that used to hold candy inside. My collection also includes an Easter wind-up toy marked "occupied Japan" that features a metal rabbit pulling a wheelbarrow that has "Happy Easter" cheerfully inscribed inside. At an estate sale, I found a celluloid rabbit, duck, and chick sitting on an egg-shaped carriage that moves forward and jingles a bell on the back when wound. A favorite in my collection is an early paper doll set of bunnies outfitted for Easter with multiple spring clothes and accouterments. My collection also includes antique, hand-painted tin Easter eggs and charming, handmade, hollow paper eggs with Easter scenes depicted inside.

Advertising giveaways frequently turn up on my search, such as a 1940s cardboard Easter folder I found with punch-out toys. I am currently searching for a few Easter toys I saw featured in a 1941 spring and Easter catalog, including a pull-toy family of waddling wooden ducks, a bunny-shaped tin wagon, and a quacking painted wooden duck pull toy. Perhaps my quest calls for another ad placed in the paper.

When my children now come to the kitchen on Easter morning, they are greeted with thick slices of French toast, Easter lilies, and a spread of some of the most interesting vintage Easter toys ever made. Although their two earlier bunnies disappeared, my children's tradition of awakening to Easter wonderment did not. To this day, the moment is just as exciting for me as it is for them.

Easter Toy Parade

If you would like to brighten your Easter basket with vintage Easter toys, the following information may be helpful.

Easter Toy History

• The Easter bunny was first mentioned in Germany in the 1500s. Children were told that if they had been good, the Easter Hare would bring them eggs.

• Many people created their own Easter toys, often from papier-mâché, until the mid-nineteenth century, when Germany became the first country to produce and export Easter toys out of such materials as composition.

• Easter was not widely celebrated in America until shortly after the Civil War.

• Stuffed toys emerged in the late 1800s, when toy manufacturers around the world began producing Easter toys and stuffed animals to boost toy sales.

• After World War I, new materials such as pressed pasteboard, tin, celluloid, and early plastics became popular choices for Easter toys. By the 1950s, most toys were either metal or plastic.

A toy Easter rabbit pushes a load of treats. Photo by Jessie Walker.

Getting Started

Your Easter toy collection can be as specific or as broad as you like, and may include:

• Stuffed animals
• Papier-mâché figurines
• Wooden pull toys
• Advertising premiums
• Children's records
• Composition figurines
• Candy containers
• Easter baskets
• Tin eggs
• Wind-up toys
• Ornaments
• Candy molds
• Tea sets
• Storybooks

What Is It Worth?

Many vintage Easter toys are priceless due to sentimental value. If you consider your collection to be a financial investment, consider the following:

• Hinged or wind-up toys should still function.

• Toys still in their original packaging will fetch higher prices.

• Rarity, age, and detail all increase a toy's value.

• Toys made by manufacturers rather than individuals are typically worth more.

• Unusual wear and tear or sloppy repairs will lower the price and value.

Toy Care and Repair

Easter toys are susceptible to damage by dust, light, and humidity. Here's how to keep your collection looking beautiful:

• For reliable repairs, take broken toys to a reputable toy restorer. A homemade repair may look satisfactory but will reduce the value of the toy.

• Dust rather than wash any stuffed treasures. This care will prolong the life of your toys.

• To prevent damage from the elements, store your vintage Easter toy collection in a glass-enclosed cabinet or under a glass garden cloche. After seasonal display, hand-wrap toys in acid-free tissue paper and store in a clean, cool, dry location.

THE EGG HUNT

Catherine Calvert

All my childhood I dreamed of an Easter egg hunt where sweets nestled behind every bush and daffodil and the trees sprouted chocolate eggs in shining foil. Even then I knew it was something of a fantasy. In Washington, D.C., where I grew up with my brother and sister, children could go roll eggs on the White House lawn, so glamorous a thought that we never did it, though we looked at the pictures of the Nixon and Eisenhower grandchildren as they rolled out the first egg. But on Easter morning our hunt was simple—finding the baskets Mother had hidden was the work of a half hour. We scoured all the familiar hiding places from the attic to the laundry room, until—"There! In the dryer!" And then we could settle down to the satisfying work of picking through the green cellophane grass, ignoring our home-dyed eggs; we'd bite the noses off marshmallow chicks and trade jelly beans. I always cornered the market in licorice ones till my basket turned black. We husbanded our loot for weeks, until marshmallows were rocklike, finally burrowing through the green shreds to find the last, lone bean sometime around the middle of May.

Like most parents, I have spent a good deal of my time ensuring that my two girls have everything I had loved and some of what I longed for. As soon as they could toddle, the ritual began. A day before Easter, the kitchen filled with that smell of eggs and vinegar. Stubby wax crayons in small fingers etched a lop-eared bunny onto a purple egg; at least as many eggs cracked and crumbled as were finally lined up in the carton, tinted those watery, tremulous colors that echo the first green shoots and tender crocuses outside. I'd read the articles about making eggs that were Michelangelo-on-the-half-shell, but we were all just as pleased with our trove of jewels bedecked with Bert and Ernie transfers.

It wasn't until I met a woman who feels about Easter the way others do about Christmas, filling the day with passion and imagination, that my childhood fantasies came pouring back. And came true. She is a person at ease with all ages, whose bright heart is written on her face; and for a dozen years she invited us to join a multitude of her friends for a grand Easter egg hunt at her Long Island farm.

> *It's an act of faith to button wriggling girls into pink cotton dresses and grandma-knit sweaters.*

Easter morning in the Northeast is, inevitably, chilly and cloudy, so it's an act of faith to button wriggling girls into pink cotton dresses and grandma-knit sweaters, while we crane to see if the sun will poke the clouds away. The new grass lies about us, a bright green that makes one blink, studded with a few hardy golden dandelions. After church (where we all come in extra strong on the hallelujahs) we are off to the hunt. As we drive in to the farm, past the woods where treasures lie, the girls squirm in their seats, baskets held tight.

Grandparents sit on the porch, aunts and uncles maneuver carriages with the newest babies, as any children old enough to walk wiggle and wait for the signal to go. But still the grown-ups cluck over how much everyone has grown, how the circle expands each year, until the children can't wait any longer. For the sake of fairness, the youngest are the first off, and the tiniest ones bumble about just a few feet away, lighting on an obvious nest with three jelly beans and a chocolate rabbit as if they've found treasure. In a moment their mouths are full of chocolate, their dresses streaked by chocolatey fingers.

I wait with the rest of the adults on the hillside, the field before us a moving patchwork of darting figures. One is wearing the cardboard bunny ears he made in kindergarten, and they wave and wiggle about the bushes. I catch a flash of pink and green, then a familiar howl—my littlest has thrust her hands into a rosebush. But she continues on, lugging her basket with its crooked bow. Through the ivy, along the drive, into the barn she goes, determined as a bee but not nearly so direct. I admire her insight. Where there are chickens,

A young girl begins her quest for eggs. Photo by Superstock.

there are bound to be eggs—though chocolate ones are unlikely.

When the platoon of older children takes off, all is purpose. For there are golden eggs to be found, and small wooden rabbits brought back from

> *My girls still talk about those days when they sailed across the muddy Long Island fields like March kites.*

Europe, and enough jelly beans to make our hostess's summer garden bloom in primary colors from undiscovered sweets. As clumps of children wander and swoop, we grown-ups keep an eye out for the unlucky ones who can't find anything but stones and have collapsed in tears in the midst of the chase. Then hand in sticky hand we go together, searching the edges and the cracks in the stone wall and the little place by the well that was never known to disappoint.

They're older now, all those children, and we live far from our friend's farm. But my teenagers still insist on dyeing a dozen or so eggs lavender and buttercup to nest in one big bowl on our dining room table. And I never neglect to buy jelly beans, because the girls give me the black ones. We still talk about those days when they sailed across the muddy Long Island fields like March kites, hot in pursuit of Easter eggs wrapped in gold, as the sun warmed at the very edge of spring. I like to think there was more gathered in those giddy childhood Easters than what filled their baskets. For a good egg-gatherer surely learns to try again, to lift her head and scan somewhere new, such as the tree branches, and to share with the others when her pile is the biggest.

Catherine Calvert, a contributing editor to Victoria *magazine, still has a fondness for marshmallow chicks.*

Ideals' Family Recipes

In honor of every child's favorite long-eared spring visitor, we've gathered a few carrot recipes that are sure to please, even if they aren't served in an Easter basket. We would love to try your favorite recipe too. Send a typed copy to Ideals Publications, 535 Metroplex Drive, Suite 250, Nashville, TN 37211. We pay $10 for each recipe published.

Carrot Cookies

Nancy Kalajainen of New Castle, Pennsylvania

2 cups all-purpose flour
2 teaspoons baking powder
¼ teaspoon salt
1 cup vegetable shortening
¾ cup granulated sugar
1 cup cooked, mashed carrots
½ cup shredded coconut
1 teaspoon vanilla
¾ cup powdered sugar
2 tablespoons milk

Preheat oven to 375° F. In a medium bowl, sift together flour, baking powder, and salt. Set aside. In a large bowl, cream shortening with sugar. Stir in carrots, coconut, and vanilla, mixing until fluffy. Slowly stir in flour mixture. Drop batter by teaspoonfuls onto a greased baking sheet. Bake 15 to 20 minutes. In a small bowl, combine powdered sugar and milk until smooth. Spoon icing over warm cookies. Makes 3 dozen cookies.

Pumpkin Carrot Raisin Bread

Anna Martin of Denver, Pennsylvania

3 cups all-purpose flour
1 tablespoon plus 2 teaspoons pumpkin pie spice
2 teaspoons baking soda
1½ teaspoons salt
3 cups granulated sugar
1 15-ounce can pumpkin
4 large eggs, slightly beaten
1 cup vegetable oil
½ cup water
1 cup shredded carrots
1 cup raisins

Preheat oven to 350° F. In a large bowl, sift together flour, pumpkin pie spice, baking soda, and salt; set aside. In a large bowl, combine sugar, pumpkin, eggs, oil, and water. Beat just until blended. Add to dry ingredients; stir just until moistened. Fold in carrots and raisins. Spoon batter into 2 greased and floured 9-by-5-inch loaf pans. Bake 60 to 65 minutes or until a toothpick inserted in the center comes out clean. Cool in pans on wire racks 10 minutes; turn out onto wire racks and cool completely. Makes 2 loaves.

Glazed Carrots

Ann Smith of Little Rock, Arkansas

1½ teaspoons butter
1 pound carrots, julienned
3 tablespoons maple syrup
⅛ teaspoon salt

In a large saucepan, drop carrots into boiling water for three minutes; drain. In a large skillet over medium-high heat, melt butter. Add carrots and sauté 1 minute. Drizzle with maple syrup and add salt. Cook, stirring constantly, until carrots are coated in glaze, approximately 2 to 3 minutes. Serve immediately. Makes 4 to 6 servings.

Carrot Casserole

Mrs. John B. Wright of Greenville, South Carolina

1 pound carrots, sliced
1 cup granulated sugar
1 stick butter, softened
3 tablespoons all-purpose flour
3 eggs, slightly beaten
1 teaspoon vanilla

In a large saucepan, place carrots. Add enough water to cover carrots, and boil until tender. Drain and mash.

Preheat oven to 350° F. Add butter and sugar to carrots; stir to melt. Stir in flour, eggs, and vanilla. Mix until smooth. Pour mixture into a greased baking dish. Bake 60 minutes or until top is crusty. Makes 6 to 8 servings.

Surprising Carrot Cake

Thelma Zook of Oakland, Maryland

2 cups all-purpose flour
2 teaspoons baking soda
1 teaspoon cinnamon
¼ teaspoon ginger
¼ teaspoon salt
3 eggs, lightly beaten
1½ cups granulated sugar
¾ cup mayonnaise
1 8-ounce can crushed pineapple, undrained
2 cups carrots, shredded
¾ cup nuts, chopped

Preheat oven to 350° F. In a medium bowl, sift together flour, baking soda, cinnamon, ginger, and salt. Set aside. In a large bowl, beat together eggs, sugar, and mayonnaise until well blended. Gradually stir in dry ingredients until well mixed. Fold in pineapple, carrots, and nuts. Spoon mixture into 2 greased and floured, 9-inch-round baking pans. Bake 30 to 35 minutes or until a toothpick inserted in the center comes out clean. Remove to wire racks to cool. Makes 8 servings.

Handmade Heirloom

Eggshell Treasures

Lisa Ragan

The humble egg has been dyed, decorated, blessed, eaten, and given at Easter for centuries. In ancient Europe, the church dictated which foods were prohibited during Lent; and since the list of forbidden foods often included eggs, Easter Sunday celebrations featured eggs on the menu in celebration of Christ's Resurrection and the end of Lenten observations. And since chickens continued to lay eggs during Lent, eggs were so plentiful that bestowing gifts of eggs on friends and family also served to distribute the abundance. Churchgoers in Slavic countries used to carry their baskets of eggs to the church to be blessed before Easter meals.

The egg has long been considered a symbol of Christ's Resurrection, although many early Europeans believed the egg did not truly symbolize the Resurrection until it was cracked open. They believed that when broken, the egg provides food for the physical self just as the body of Jesus was broken to provide "food" for the spiritual self.

An ancient Russian custom included the practice of giving guests an egg on Easter in commemoration of the Resurrection of Christ. The custom also included visiting friends and family on Easter and bestowing upon them gifts of eggs. In the late 1880s, this Russian tradition of egg gifts inspired Carl Fabergé, the court jeweler to the Tsar of Russia, to create elaborate golden eggs encrusted with jewels that he presented to the Tsar himself. Members of the royal Russian family were so delighted with the bejeweled eggs that they began commissioning Fabergé to design even more eggs. Fabergé often designed the eggs to contain surprises inside such as a tiny golden hen with rubies for eyes or tiny cameos of the Russian royal children. Many of these famous jeweled eggs can be seen today in museums around the world.

Although Fabergé enjoyed the luxury of crafting eggs out of precious metals and gemstones, today's egg artisans use organic hollowed eggs to create Fabergé-inspired Easter gifts that can be cherished for generations to come. Some of these egg creations are simple, painted shells with windows offering views of tiny Easter scenes. More elaborate eggs open to reveal music boxes or clocks, and there are even large ostrich eggs cut and decorated to resemble Cinderella's majestic coach.

Directions on how to make decorative hol-

> *Egg-giving at Eastertime continues a long-held tradition of sharing abundant gifts in honor of Christ's Resurrection.*

lowed eggs can be found in craft books or classes. Many interested crafters prefer to find an experienced egg artist and learn firsthand. The first step in making a hollowed egg is to select an egg. Several different types of eggs can be used, including ostrich, emu, rhea, goose, duck, and chicken. Egg artisans recommend obtaining organic eggs from birds that have not been fed antibiotics, since organic eggs tend to have thicker, stronger shells with more even shapes. Ostrich eggs offer the largest size of egg and feature an interesting, dimpled surface. Duck eggs, in contrast, have especially smooth shells and are sturdier than chicken eggs.

Hollowed eggs can be purchased at florist supply shops or specialty craft stores, or eggs can be hollowed at home following directions found in craft books or classes. Once rinsed and dried, the hollowed eggs can be held with a thin knitting needle or meat skewer during the decorating process.

Some artisans coat the exterior of the hollowed egg with epoxy to reduce the risk of breakage while creating an opening. Using one's fingers, small manicure scissors, or kitchen scissors, carefully create an opening in the egg, breaking off small bits of shell at a time. The opening can be left slightly jagged for an interesting, just-cracked effect; or the edges can be sanded down smooth. Some crafters choose to cover the edges of the opening with ribbon, trimming, or beads.

For a smooth, perfect opening, many artisans use a high-speed rotary tool with a diamond tip; this method offers more possibilities of opening shapes, such as an arched window, a perfect oval, or even a hinged door. The hollowed egg can then be dyed, painted, or decorated in any desired manner.

To add a tiny surprise in the hollowed egg in the manner of Fabergé, fill the bottom of the hollowed egg with plaster of Paris and place in an empty egg carton to dry. The plaster of Paris will create a flat surface upon which to arrange a miniature scene or tiny bouquet. Traditional Easter designs and symbols include a crown of thorns, cross, chalice, lamb, lilies, or angels. Pastoral themes might include a tree, a swimming swan, long-tailed birds, or a tiny hatchling in a nest. Hollowed egg crafters often use wood or plastic miniatures or a variety of found objects to create scenes. Some artisans even create pomanders of potpourri or elegant jewelry cases from hollowed eggs.

Since eggshell is a natural material, it will decompose if not properly sealed after decorating. The finished hollowed egg should be painted with a clear matte or gloss ceramic sealer or an acrylic or polyurethane coating to prevent decomposition.

Egg-giving at Eastertime continues a long-held tradition of sharing abundant gifts in honor of Christ's Resurrection. Although most of today's crafters may not be able to create eggs of gold and precious jewels as did Carl Fabergé, they are able to transform humble, ordinary eggs into elegant keepsakes. And it is these keepsakes that honor the Christian faith through an artistic endeavor worthy of becoming a family heirloom.

Humble eggshells can become an ornate clock such as this one. Photo by Robin Conover.

The Secret

Daniel Whitehead Hicky

They cannot know a secret that I know,
The city dwellers with their leaden eyes,
Caught like a leaf in traffic's ebb and flow,
Deafened by all a city's raucous cries;
They cannot know it in the canyons there
Where steel and stone deflect a mortal's stare.

For I arose before the moon went down,
Halfway toward morning.
    Dew-wet lay the world
And, in the sunrise, brighter than the town.
Deep in the valley's hush, I found uncurled
A bloodroot flower;
    I touched it with my hand,
And I alone knew spring was on the land.

Wasted Hours

Edgar Daniel Kramer

Folks say that I have wasted many hours
In loitering along a lilac lane,
In sprawling on a hilltop sweet with flowers,
In wandering through mists of summer rain.

Long since they sighed
    and left me to my dreaming;
He will not plow who walks to meet the moon,
Who whispers to the wan stars softly gleaming
And hearkens to the songs the fairies croon.

Folks shake their heads
    but, oh, they are not knowing,
As in the beaten paths they trudge and plod,
That in these wasted hours I am going
With beauty in the ways that lead to God.

Yellow fawn lilies spread over a field in Montana's Glacier National Park. Photo by ImageState/Alpen Image, Ltd. Inset: A bloodroot flower reveals its simple beauty in Kewaunee County, Wisconsin. Photo by Darryl R. Beers.

Hills in Spring

Jessie Wilmore Murton

Surely God must have walked among these hills!
The stately steppings of His holy feet
Are imprinted on each wild and barren crag
And echo through each cool and dim retreat.

Here, singing streams in joyful symphonies
Their praiseful chants and litanies repeat;
Here, from the depths of green and cloistered aisles,
Pale-petaled urns dispense their incense sweet;

And lifting up the eyes to gaze upon
This calm blue peace, this everlasting strength,
One senses He whose footsteps linger here
Will answer all life's questioning at length.

*Oaks seem to tumble down the hills in
California's Mount Diablo State Park.
Photo by Carr Clifton.*

From My Garden Journal

TRILLIUM

Lisa Ragan

For many people, gardening constitutes a spiritual experience that includes ardent prayer and quiet time with the Creator, as well as joyful thanksgiving and praise. And oh, how the hosannas do ring as the first spring blossoms appear! When I spy those brave little flowers shooting up from the cold earth, I am reminded again of the promise of the Resurrection at Easter.

One special blossom that acts as both a harbinger of spring and a symbol of the Holy Trinity is the humble trillium, a herbaceous perennial that carpets forest floors throughout many cooler regions of North America. Named for its three petals and three leaves, the trillium provides a beautiful representation of the three parts to the Holy Trinity. Also called the wake robin, this little plant signals the start of spring as its snowy white bloom with a buttery yellow center unfolds against rich green foliage. Perhaps the nickname wake robin, which has also been applied to numerous other plants, refers to the trillium's shared role with the robin as heralds of spring.

Primarily a North American species, the trillium grows abundantly throughout Canada and

> As I take my annual first-day-of-spring walk, I enjoy scanning the woodland floor for a simple white wildflower with a powerful message.

the northeastern United States and is also found, though less abundantly, in gardens of more temperate regions. The trillium's signature, three-petaled flower and whorl of three elliptical leaves radiate from a short rootstock, which keeps the plant rather low growing. The trillium typically grows to heights between six and eighteen inches and spreads approximately one foot. Relying heavily on the insect world, the plants are pollinated by honeybees, bumblebees, and a variety of beetles. In addition, the trillium owes its dispersal in part to ants and wasps, which eat part of the trillium seed and then disperse the main seed throughout their habitats.

The trillium's single flower appears in spring and doesn't stay for long. The most well-known variety is White Trillium, *trillium grandiflorum,* which produces soft white flowers that can span from three to seven inches across and will blush a soft pink just before wilting. Some specimens have double flower forms and mottled green leaves. Trillium plants sleep the summer away after they shed their leaves; and although the blooming season ends far too soon, trillium plants require very little maintenance to keep the flowers coming year after year.

More than forty trillium species are native to North America, with a few in northeastern Asia and the Himalayas. Cultivars of *trillium grandiflorum* include *Florepleno* (a double-flowered variety in the traditional white) and *Roseum* (also a double-flowered variety but in a pink hue). Other varieties include *trillium cernuum* (hanging trillium), *trillium erectum* (a red trillium with a strong, disagreeable odor), *trillium undulatum* (a trillium with especially wavy leaves), *trillium luteum* (a lovely yellow variety), and *trillium sessile* (which has a striking, deep maroon flower).

A perennial grown from bulb-like rhizomes, trilliums grow well in partial shade, ideally beneath leafy canopies. In the wild, one can often find trilliums amid stands of maples. Experts do not recommend that wild specimens be pilfered from their natural habitat; instead, trilliums should be purchased from a reputable nursery. Take note, however, that propagated plants will be small. Trilliums thrive in rich, fertile soil that is complemented with compost annually. In mid- to late-autumn, plant the trillium rhizome four to six inches deep in moist soil with adequate drainage. Trillium seeds can be sown when they ripen in early summer, but plants purchased from a nursery produce faster results. If sown from seed, trilliums will first produce a one-leafed plant with no flower. The plant will gradu-

ally mature and after five to seven years, produce its first blossom. Trilliums can be propagated by carefully dividing the root in late summer or early autumn after the trillium has shed its leaves, although some experts recommend leaving plants intact for best growth.

The trillium is quite hardy and resistant to most pests and diseases. Young trillium plants can be susceptible to hungry snails and slugs, but mature plants can generally withstand a typical mollusk onslaught. Humans have unfortunately threatened the health of some trillium species by clear-cutting forests and altering their native habitats. Clear-cutting companies often replace the downed trees with conifers, which create a more acidic soil environment that is less conducive to trillium populations.

An interesting fact about the trillium is that one can estimate the plant's age by inspecting the rhizome. Like counting the concentric rings on a tree stump, one can count the number of constrictions on the trillium's rhizome. Each constriction (a ring around the rhizome that looks almost as though someone has tightened a piece of string around it) represents roughly one year. Individual plants have been known to live as long as seventy years.

As I take my annual first-day-of-spring walk, I enjoy scanning the woodland floor for a simple white wildflower with a powerful message. Its blossoms remind me that spring has come; and with it comes a time to celebrate the message of the Holy Trinity and the promise of the Resurrection.

Lisa Ragan tends her small but mighty city garden in Nashville, Tennessee, with the help of her two Shih Tzu puppies, Clover and Curry.

Faith Reborn

Constance Cullingworth

Climb a hill in April,
Walk a country lane,
Bend to touch a primrose—
Find your faith again.

Pause to watch a wild bird,
Thrill to hear him sing,
Lift your eyes to heaven—
Faith returns in spring.

Blade and leaf, bush and tree
Cast off the old and worn,
Robe themselves in beauty—
A sign of faith reborn.

So God works His wonders,
And every living thing
Rejoices that a sleeping faith
Awakens with the spring.

**Faith is the root;
hope is the stem;
love is the perfect flower.**
—F. B. MEYER

*Showy primroses create a pink carpet in a yard in
Gastonia, North Carolina. Photo by Norman Poole.*

Easter Promise
Helen Williams

Remember that although the world
Once witnessed Friday's cross,
The promised joy of Easter came
To end that night of loss;
So that the Resurrection morn
Would never fail to be
The light of life that always robs
The grave of victory.

Bless Us, Lord
Nancy Byrd Turner

In a sweet springtime
Half the world away,
Jesus Christ arose for us
At the break of day.

Now again it's springtime—
Bending low we pray,
Bless us, Lord of Easter,
On Thy Easter Day!

My Easter Wish
Author Unknown

May the glad dawn
Of Easter morn
Bring joy to thee.
May the calm eve
Of Easter leave
A peace divine with thee.
May Easter night
On thine heart write,
O Christ, I live for Thee.

An Easter Song
Susan Coolidge

A song of sunshine through the rain,
Of spring across the snow;
A balm to heal the hurts of pain,
A peace surpassing woe.
Lift up your heads, ye sorrowing ones,
And be ye glad at heart.
For Calvary and Easter Day,
Earth's saddest day and gladdest day,
Were just three days apart!

*Spring offers purple and white gifts from the
garden. Photo by Nancy Matthews.*

Devotions FROM THE Heart

Pamela Kennedy

And he went a little farther, and fell on His face, and prayed, saying, O my Father, if it be possible, let this cup pass from me: nevertheless not as I will, but as thou wilt.—Matthew 26:39

FATHER KNOWS BEST

When our daughter received the long-awaited letter announcing her dorm and roommate assignments for her first year in college, she couldn't wait to read the news. She had been assured that her early acceptance at the university guaranteed her first choice of a double room in her preferred dorm. As she ripped open the letter and scanned it, I watched her expression change from one of happy anticipation to disappointment. Yes, she had been placed in her dorm of choice, but was assigned with two other girls to a twelve-by-nineteen-foot triple room.

"Mom, how are we ever going to get all our stuff into that tiny space? It's so hard with three—someone always gets left out. This is going to be a mess. It's not at all what I expected!"

I responded with motherly platitudes about looking on the bright side, how fun it would be to have two roomies instead of just one, how it would be a good time for learning to compromise and to learn to live in harmony. I could tell she wasn't buying my Pollyanna philosophy.

"Well," I admitted. "It's not what I had hoped would happen either. But perhaps God has a reason for it. Would you be willing to look at it from that angle?"

She sighed and said, "I guess I might as well. There's nothing I can do about it anyway. I just hope He knows what He's doing!"

Our conversation came back to me at Easter when I read again the account of our Lord's last days on earth. Time and again the ways that seemed best from a human perspective were frustrated. When the delegation came to arrest Jesus, Peter leapt forward in an attempt to protect the Lord and sliced off the ear of one of the men. Rebuking the impulsive disciple, Jesus healed the severed ear and said, in essence, that God had a different plan. Later, in Gethsemane, after earnest prayers that God would provide Him an escape from the path of suffering, the Lord humbly submitted to the Father's will over His own. Even when the crowds taunted Him to come down and prove His divinity, He resolutely remained on the cross, forgiving their arrogance, knowing that was God's way to offer the proof they demanded. And

Dear Lord, when I do not understand why things happen the way they do, help me rest in the knowledge that Your will is always best. Amen.

at the end, when His enemies had done everything humanly possible to eliminate Him, He arose and returned offering eternal life.

Over and over again the Scriptures teach us that our ways are not God's ways; when we are weak, He is strong; and when we are lost, His grace finds us. When we have problems and challenges, we often see no way out. Our perspective is earthbound by what we know of probabilities and past experiences. But God's view is eternal. Knowing the end from the beginning and unlimited by time and space, His wisdom is infinite. The challenge for us is to trust Him more than we trust ourselves—to be willing to accept that our vision is not always clear, our perspective not always correct. There are times when we are certain our lives have taken a wrong turn only to discover that what we thought was a burden, God turned into a blessing. At other times our sorrow is so great we doubt God's grace can reach us; then like the sunrise on that first Easter morning, His light gently penetrates the places of our deepest grief. And even in our everyday moments when we can't seem to figure out what life is all about, we can rest in the confidence that He does.

The first day of her college career our daughter moved into that tiny dorm room with two other college freshmen. They struggled with closet space and sleeping schedules and learned to respect one another's likes and dislikes. They were sometimes frustrated with each other and came to understand forgiveness and grace and the power of laughter and love. Her second year she was assigned to a double room and joyfully anticipated the luxury of a little more space and just one roommate. But if I asked her what she learned from her freshman experience, I suspect

Symbols of the season are gathered by photographer Nancy Matthews.

she would quickly respond that, despite her doubts, her heavenly Father really did know what He was doing.

Pamela Kennedy is a freelance writer of short stories, articles, essays, and children's books. Wife of a retired naval officer and mother of three children, she has made her home on both U.S. coasts and currently resides in Honolulu, Hawaii.

Once in a Garden
William Arnette Wofford

Once in a garden, long ago,
One prayed in His extremity.
The fragrant hyacinth nearby
Leaned close to give Him sympathy.

The tiny lily of the field
Glowed like a pure white candle there
And gently touched Him where He knelt
And agonized alone in prayer.

The blossoms of the flowering thorn
Looked on the sorrow in His face
And sought to shield the Son of God
From sharp thorns in that lonely place.

Oft had they seen the Master come
At morn or in the moonlight's glow;
And after He communed with God,
His smile revealed He loved them so.

The lily, hyacinth, and thorn
Kept watch within the shadows dim.
And when their friend was led away,
They bowed their heads and wept for Him.

*Easter lilies and pink hyacinths form an Easter
still life. Photo by Norman Poole.*

35

THE LAST SUPPER

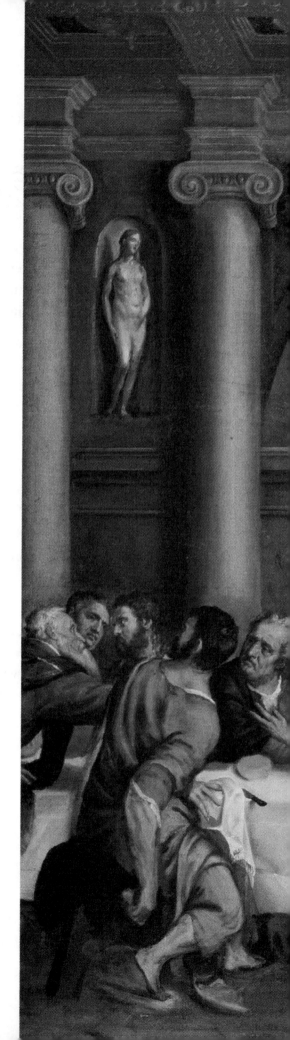

ow the first day of the feast of unleavened bread the disciples came to Jesus, saying unto him, Where wilt thou that we prepare for thee to eat the passover?

And he said, Go into the city to such a man, and say unto him, The Master saith, My time is at hand; I will keep the passover at thy house with my disciples.

And the disciples did as Jesus had appointed them; and they made ready the passover.

Now when the even was come, he sat down with the twelve. . . . And as they were eating, Jesus took bread, and blessed it, and brake it, and gave it to the disciples, and said, Take, eat; this is my body.

And he took the cup, and gave thanks, and gave it to them, saying, Drink ye all of it; For this is my blood of the new testament, which is shed for many for the remission of sins. But I say unto you, I will not drink henceforth of this fruit of the vine, until that day when I drink it new with you in my Father's kingdom.

MATTHEW 26:17–20, 26–29

OIL SKETCH FOR THE LAST SUPPER by Titian (c. 1488–1576). Image from Pinacoteca di Brera, Milan, Italy. Cameraphoto/Art Resource, New York.

THE CROWN OF THORNS

And straightway in the morning the chief priests held a consultation with the elders and scribes and the whole council, and bound Jesus, and carried him away, and delivered him to Pilate. And Pilate asked him, Art thou the King of the Jews?

And he answering said unto him, Thou sayest it.

Now at that feast he released unto them one prisoner, whomsoever they desired. And there was one named Barabbas . . . who had committed murder in the insurrection.

And Pilate answered and said again unto them, What will ye then that I shall do unto him whom ye call the King of the Jews? And they cried out again, Crucify him.

Then Pilate said unto them, Why, what evil hath he done?

And they cried out the more exceedingly, Crucify him.

And so Pilate, willing to content the people, released Barabbas unto them, and delivered Jesus, when he had scourged him, to be crucified.

And the soldiers led him away into the hall. . . . And they clothed him with purple, and platted a crown of thorns, and put it about his head, And began to salute him, Hail, King of the Jews! And they smote him on the head with a reed, and did spit upon him, and bowing their knees worshipped him. And when they had mocked him, they took off the purple from him, and put his own clothes on him, and led him out to crucify him.

MARK 15:1, 2, 6, 7, 12–20

CHRIST CROWNED WITH THORNS by Titian (c. 1488–1576). Image from R. G. Ojeda. Louvre, Paris, France. Réunion des Musées Nationaux/Art Resource, New York.

THE CROSS

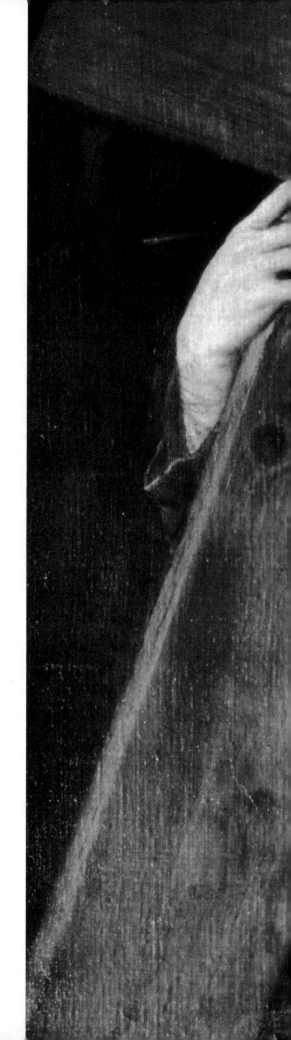

 nd they bring him unto the place Golgotha, which is, being interpreted, The place of a skull. And they gave him to drink wine mingled with myrrh: but he received it not.

And when they had crucified him, they parted his garments, casting lots upon them, what every man should take. And it was the third hour, and they crucified him. And the superscription of his accusation was written over, THE KING OF THE JEWS.

And with him they crucify two thieves; the one on his right hand, and the other on his left. And the scripture was fulfilled, which saith, And he was numbered with the transgressors. . . .

And when the sixth hour was come, there was darkness over the whole land until the ninth hour. And at the ninth hour Jesus cried with a loud voice, saying, *Eloi, Eloi, lama sabachthani?* which is, being interpreted, My God, my God, why hast thou forsaken me?

And some of them that stood by, when they heard it, said, Behold, he calleth Elias. And one ran and filled a sponge full of vinegar, and put it on a reed, and gave him to drink, saying, Let alone; let us see whether Elias will come to take him down.

And Jesus cried with a loud voice, and gave up the ghost. And the veil of the temple was rent in twain from the top to the bottom.

And when the centurion, which stood over against him, saw that he so cried out, and gave up the ghost, he said, Truly this man was the Son of God.

MARK 15:22–28, 33–39

CHRIST AND SIMON THE CYRENIAN by Titian (c. 1488–1576). Image from Superstock.

THE SUPPER AT EMMAUS

nd, behold, two of them went that same day to a village called Emmaus. . . . And they talked together of all these things which had happened.

And it came to pass, that, while they communed together and reasoned, Jesus himself drew near, and went with them. But their eyes were holden that they should not know him. And he said unto them, What manner of communications are these that ye have one to another, as ye walk, and are sad?

And the one of them, whose name was Cleopas, answering said unto him, Art thou only a stranger in Jerusalem, and hast not known the things which are come to pass there in these days?

And he said unto them, What things?

And they said unto him, Concerning Jesus of Nazareth, which was a prophet mighty in deed and word before God and all the people: And how the chief priests and our rulers delivered him to be condemned to death, and have crucified him. . . .

And they drew nigh unto the village . . . and he made as though he would have gone further. But they constrained him, saying, Abide with us: for it is toward evening, and the day is far spent. And he went in to tarry with them. And it came to pass, as he sat at meat with them, he took bread, and blessed it, and brake, and gave to them.

And their eyes were opened, and they knew him; and he vanished out of their sight. . . . And they rose up the same hour, and returned to Jerusalem, and found the eleven gathered together, and them that were with them, Saying, The Lord is risen indeed.

LUKE 24:13–20, 28–34

THE SUPPER AT EMMAUS by Titian (c. 1488–1576). Image from R. G. Ojeda. Louvre, Paris, France. Réunion des Musées Nationaux/Art Resource, New York.

THE ASCENSION

And he said unto them, These are the words which I spake unto you, while I was yet with you, that all things must be fulfilled, which were written in the law of Moses, and in the prophets, and in the psalms, concerning me.

Then opened he their understanding, that they might understand the scriptures, And said unto them, Thus it is written, and thus it behoved Christ to suffer, and to rise from the dead the third day: And that repentance and remission of sins should be preached in his name among all nations, beginning at Jerusalem. And ye are witnesses of these things.

And, behold, I send the promise of my Father upon you: but tarry ye in the city of Jerusalem, until ye be endued with power from on high.

And he led them out as far as to Bethany, and he lifted up his hands, and blessed them. And it came to pass, while he blessed them, he was parted from them, and carried up into heaven.

And they worshipped him, and returned to Jerusalem with great joy: And were continually in the temple, praising and blessing God. Amen.

LUKE 24:44–53

Glory, Laud, Honor

Theodulf of Orleans

All glory, laud, and honor
To You, Redeemer King!
To whom the lips of children
Made sweet hosannas ring.

You are the King of Israel
And David's royal Son,
Now in the Lord's name coming,
Our King and blessed One.

The company of angels
Are praising You on high;
And mortals, joined with all things
Created, make reply.

The people of the Hebrews
With palms before You went;
Our praise and prayers and anthems
Before You we present.

To You before Your passion
They sang their hymns of praise;
To You, now high exalted,
Our melody we raise.

Their praises You accepted;
Accept the prayers we bring,
Great source of love and goodness,
Our Saviour and our King.

Blessing and Honor

Horatius Bonar

Blessing and honor and glory and power,
Wisdom and riches and strength evermore,
Give ye to Him who our battle hath won,
Whose are the kingdom, the crown, and the throne.

Dwelleth the light of the glory with Him,
Light of a glory that cannot grow dim,
Light in its silence and beauty and calm,
Light in its gladness and brightness and balm.

Ever ascendeth the song and the joy;
Ever descendeth the love from on high.
Blessing and honor and glory and praise,
This is the theme of the hymns that we raise.

Life of all life, and true Light of all light,
Star of the dawning, unchangingly bright,
Sing we the song of the Lamb that was slain,
Dying in weakness, but rising to reign.

A church steeple is framed with apple blossoms in North Carolina's Blue Ridge Mountains. Photo by Norman Poole.

THROUGH MY WINDOW

NEVER TOO LATE

Pamela Kennedy

My life was one of conflict. Torn between my hesitancy and a desire to act upon my convictions, I walked a tightrope between cowardice and courage, struggling to be free from guilt. And then one day, convinced I had missed my last opportunity for inner peace, I learned a lesson only God could teach.

Like my heart, Jerusalem was a place of contradiction. In the polished courts of the temple, priests in jeweled robes accepted offerings from those seeking forgiveness while the oily smoke from their sacrificial fires seeped into dingy alleys. Beggars reached out gnarled hands for mercy as busy lawyers, on their way to argue for justice, swept past without a glance. And I, Joseph of Arimathea, a member of the Jewish Supreme Court, spent my life debating legal minutiae.

It was within this court, the Sanhedrin, that the seeds of both my cowardice and courage

took root. A debate had raged for months over the recent popularity of a man some claimed to be the Messiah. Most of my colleagues found these claims blasphemous and the man Himself worthy of death. Additionally, they felt a personal threat as He taught a doctrine at odds with the ancient ways, threatening destruction on us religious leaders for our corruption of God's Law.

The problem was with the people. He was immensely popular, and hundreds followed Him everywhere as each week brought new accounts of his miracles, healings, and exorcisms. In our chamber the heated debate continued as one after another rose to express contempt for this itinerant, uneducated rabbi from Nazareth. Unwilling to cast an uninformed ballot, I determined to investigate the troublemaker for myself.

Day after day I stood with the rabble surrounding Jesus, listening to His teaching, watching His face, examining His interaction with the people clamoring for His attention. And day by day I became more convinced that this uneducated rabbi was unique. He spoke with authority about forgiveness and reconciliation, healing and compassion. He urged His followers to obey the spirit, not just the words, of the ancient Law and to be willing to lay down their lives for their friends. He was patient and kind, but never weak.

And as I listened, something burned within my heart. It dawned on me that He did more than just speak the truth; I realized He *was* the Truth.

But what could I do? My peers had made their positions clear. I risked expulsion from the Sanhedrin by siding with this rebel. The ancient traditions of my culture bound me tighter than my newfound hope. Tentative, I spoke privately to a colleague who had once stood before the Council

---

He did more than just speak the truth; I realized He was the Truth.

---

suggesting we ignore this so-called prophet, until time proved Him either true or false. Placing his arm about my shoulders, Nicodemus related a midnight conversation with Jesus. He said the man had spoken to him of a new birth only experienced by those with true faith. His heart was as moved as mine he said; but like myself, he remained silent. What could it hurt to wait just a little longer?

Then, one night during Passover week, the president of the Sanhedrin called an emergency meeting. In a frenzy born of desperate fear and anger, arguments echoed through the chamber. "He must be stopped!" "The people are ready to declare Him King!" "The Romans will kill us all!" "Better one to die than everyone!"

Suddenly I stood, found my voice, and loudly cast my vote against the majority. Shocked silence, then murmurs, then shouting swallowed up my plea. It was too late. In a few moments it was over. The condemnation held, and those thirsty for blood ran from the chamber to plead their case before the Roman procurator, Pilate.

Scarcely twelve hours later, I stood on a small hillside called Golgotha and watched the Son of God die on a wooden cross. Once more I was silent, strangled this time by guilt. I watched the sky turn dark, women weeping, soldiers gambling for His only piece of clothing. And I heard the words that still whisper in my soul: "Father forgive them." I knew they were meant for me. The earth heaved with anguish and a voice cried, "It is finished."

Screaming as if in pain, I ran to Pilate's courtyard, beat upon the locked gates, and insisted on an audience before the proconsul.

"Give me the body of the Christ!" I demanded.

Unwilling to meet Jesus while He lived, I could now only reach out to Him in death. Pilate's signed permission in hand, I ran to fetch Nicodemus, and together we raced back to the hill outside the city to claim the body of the Lord.

We lifted the lifeless form from the cross and tenderly wrapped it in strips of fine, clean linen. Then, bearing the body I knew I had helped to slay, I placed it in the tomb prepared for my own burial. Silently we backed out of the limestone cave, sealing the opening with a huge boulder.

I returned to my home heavy with self-condemnation and regret and fell upon my bed. It was there Nicodemus found me the morning after the Sabbath. Excited, he told me of the miracle reported by the women. Together we raced to see for ourselves and found it was just as they had said: The boulder was moved! The tomb was empty!

In the weeks that followed, we saw the risen Christ, walked with Him, and finally understood the ancient promises of God with hearts reborn. It was then I realized that overshadowing all my failure is His victory and the blessed assurance that I am beloved by God, forever forgiven. It was then I learned the lesson of the Resurrection: With God, it is never too late.

Pamela Kennedy is a freelance writer of short stories, articles, essays, and children's books. Wife of a retired naval officer and mother of three children, she has made her home on both U.S. coasts and currently resides in Honolulu, Hawaii.

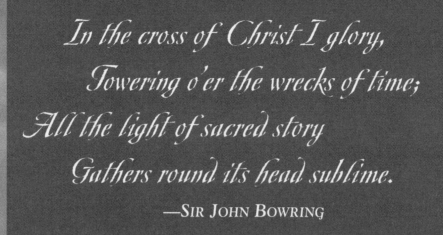

In the cross of Christ I glory,
Towering o'er the wrecks of time;
All the light of sacred story
Gathers round its head sublime.

—SIR JOHN BOWRING

The Meeting

John D. Womack

The lady looked so sweet, yet sad somehow—
The one I met upon the street today.
She stopped and gazed at me, and smoothed my brow,
And murmured to herself, "This is the way
He looked, my very own, with curls just so."
I couldn't help but wonder whom she meant.
She kissed me on the cheek and turned to go;
I heard a quiet sobbing as she went.

I wonder who she was. She had the air
Of one who'd had a task and done it well
And never questioned whether it was fair
It should be hers to do, though I could tell
The doing put her near despair. Oh, still:
They've crucified three men upon Golgotha hill.

The sun rises over New Hampshire's White
Mountain National Forest. Photo by William
H. Johnson/Johnson's Photography.

Maker of Heaven and Earth

Cecil Frances Alexander

All things bright and beautiful,
All creatures great and small,
All things wise and wonderful,
The Lord God made them all.

Each little flower that opens,
Each little bird that sings,
He made their glowing colors;
He made their tiny wings.

The rich man in his castle,
The poor man at his gate,
God made them, high or lowly,
And ordered their estate.

The purple-headed mountain,
The river running by,
The sunset and the morning
That brightens up the sky,

The cold wind in the winter,
The pleasant summer sun,
The ripe fruits in the garden—
He made them, every one.

The tall trees in the green wood,
The meadows where we play,
The rushes by the water
We gather every day.

He gave us eyes to see them,
And lips that we might tell
How great is God Almighty
Who has made all things well.

*Monkey flowers grow beside a creek near
Washington's Mount Rainier. Photo by Dennis Frates.*

An April Morning

Bliss Carman

Once more in misted April
The world is growing green;
Along the winding river
The plumey willows lean.

Beyond the sweeping meadows
The looming mountains rise
Like battlements of dreamland
Against the brooding skies.

The golden wings and bluebirds
Call to their heavenly choirs.
The pines are blued and drifted
With smoke of brushwood fires.

And in my sister's garden
Where little breezes run,
The golden daffodillies
Are blowing in the sun.

April Promise

Mary E. Linton

I think the world was born one April day
With fragrant winds astir upon the deep,
With bursting blossoms and the first bright ray
Of sunlight bringing life to powers asleep.
Out of primeval fire, the earth we know
Blossomed with gentle warmth one April dawn,
Burst softly into time as petals glow
With newborn rapture on a dew-kissed lawn.
And every year it celebrates anew,
Small candles bright with yellow jonquil flame.
Oh, happy birthday, all the world, to you!
What joy to be alive and call your name.
What joy to share with you another year
When blossoms rich with promise reappear.

*Multi-colored lilies sweeten a brick path in British
Columbia, Canada. Photo by Dennis Frates.*

Growth
Lucille Veneklasen

There is such beauty in the pulsing strength
Of growing things—
The vibrant greenness of a shoot to which
The soil still clings,
The lacy edges of a tiny leaf
So late uncurled,
A sturdy stem which stands erect to view
Its strange new world.

In Every Growing Thing
Duane Mars Davis

But now, at last, I have escaped my bonds;
I can go wandering by moonlit ponds
And rivers in the cool of night
Or in the morning, in the first, fresh light,
Retake my soul into the sunlit dawn,
Absorb the radiance of the golden spring,
And find our God in every growing thing.

Lord, make us mindful of the
little things that grow and blossom
in these days to make the world
beautiful for us.—W. E. DuBois

*Border: Hosta foliage sports its best spring green in
Multnomah County, Oregon. Photo by Steve Terrill.
Right: A trio of crown vetch blossoms reaches
toward the spring sun. Photo by Darryl R. Beers.*

FOR THE CHILDREN

Springtime

Nikki Giovanni

in springtime the violets
grow in the sidewalk cracks
and the ants play furiously
at my gym-shoed toes
carrying off a half-eaten peanut
butter sandwich I had at lunch
and sometimes I crumble
my extra graham crackers
and on the rainy days I take off
my yellow space hat and splash
all the puddles on Pendry Street
   and not one
cold can catch me.

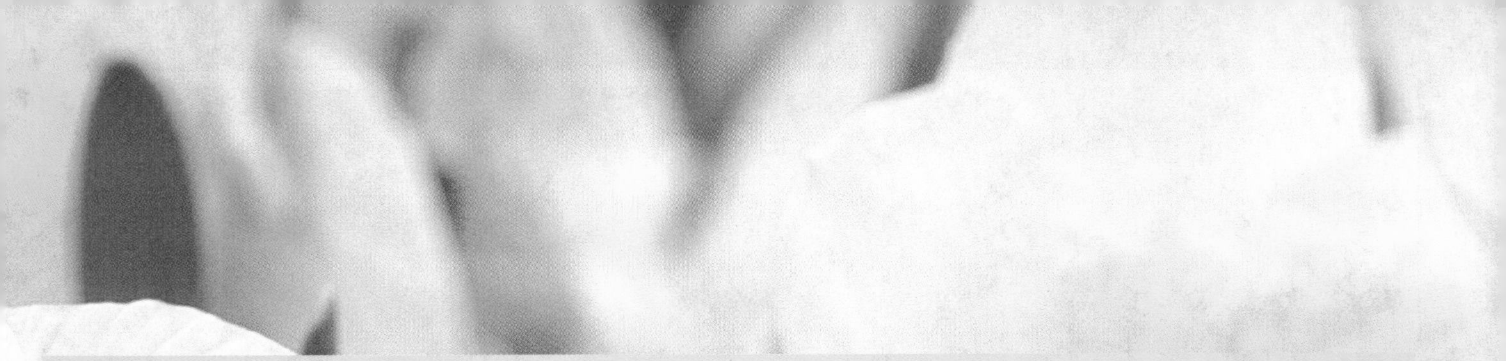

Buds and Bonnets

Esther Kem Thomas

How can I fret at the fate of the nation
Or keep a world crisis in focus
When out on the lawn is a gay situation
Involving a new Easter crocus?

How could I call all my worries together
Or think, but in words of a sonnet,
When song is inspired by this blue and gold weather
And I've a brand-new Easter bonnet?

How could I doubt a worldwide resurrection
When winterlike dying is through
And living is tinged with a mirrored reflection
Of everything budding anew?

Let me sing on of an ultimate rightness;
Let me believe in a sonnet;
Let me wear faith like a garment of brightness,
Topped off with a new Easter bonnet!

*Hybrid daffodils bloom in Door County,
Wisconsin. Photo by Darryl R. Beers.
Inset: A young girl shows off her best Easter
bonnet and bouquet. Photo by Superstock.*

*From childhood's garden
of flowers and lace
And an angel smile
upon each face.*

Easter Bouquet

Beverly J. Anderson

A vision of spring passed my way
In form of an Eastertime bouquet—
Forget-me-nots of powder blue,
Roses sweet of every hue,
Daffodils of sunny gold,
All so lovely to behold.
Lavender lilacs, daisies of white,
Tulips too in colors bright,
Pink sweet peas, and pansies gay
All on parade this Easter Day.
From childhood's garden of flowers and lace
And an angel smile upon each face—
Joyful, frilly little girls
With shining eyes and golden curls
Form an Eastertime bouquet,
Dressed in Sunday school array.

White-Petaled Laughter

Betty W. Stoffel

Magnolia trees that lined the street
Stood silent all year long,
Tight-lipped against the winter,
Too chilled for merry song.

Then furtively small buds broke out
In mild contagious mirth,
And suddenly burst forth so loud
They fairly shook the earth.

From tree to tree the volatile joy
Exploded gaily after
And shook the roots of early spring
In full, white-petaled laughter.

*A star magnolia in Madison, Wisconsin,
showers the grass with snow-white petals.
Photo by Darryl R. Beers.*

GLENN MILLER

Patricia A. Pingry

During the 1930s, tanks swept much of Europe, families lined up at public soup kitchens, and the Midwest blew itself into a great dustbowl. Into the midst of this unhappy world came the sound of big bands playing the fast tempo of "swing." Kids flocked to the dance floor to jitterbug their cares away to the sounds of Benny Goodman, Tommy and Jimmy Dorsey, and Artie Shaw. But the most successful big band of them all—voted number one from 1939 to 1941—was the band of Glenn Miller.

BUILDING A BAND

During these years, Glenn Miller's "sound" wafted over the radio waves almost continuously, from both disc jockeys playing his recordings as well as the broadcast of Miller's band's own radio show. Songs like "Kalamazoo," "String of Pearls," "Don't Sit Under the Apple Tree," "Chattanooga Choo Choo," and "Moonlight Serenade" became huge hits; and Miller's recording of "Tuxedo Junction" broke records in its first week of release. Heard at Carnegie Hall, at state fairs, and on movie soundtracks, Glenn Miller's band became so popular that by 1941 its weekly take was $20,000—an unheard-of sum during these years. But the money and the applause from his fans weren't enough for Miller. He had been on the USO circuit and came to believe that "the most important sound that can possibly come out of concerts [is] the sound of thousands of G.I.'s reacting with an ear-splitting, almost hysterical happy yell after each number."

BIRTH OF A BAND LEADER

Alton Glenn Miller was born in the tiny town of Clarinda, Iowa, on March 1, 1904, to Mattie Lou Cavender and Elmer Miller. After two moves, the family settled in Fort Morgan, Colorado.

No one really knows what propelled Miller toward music. Their early home had an organ that Mattie played, and the Miller legend has the family singing during their trips to and from town in the family horse-drawn wagon. In high school, Miller acquired a trombone and joined the band. Although he was a good football player, by the time he attended the University of Colorado, music had replaced sports. "I excelled in football, but fear of injury to my mouth kept me out of college competition."

LOOKING FOR A "SOUND"

Miller briefly attended the University of Colorado, but he lacked the finances and the desire to continue, for his heart and ambitions were set on music. By the age of twenty-two, he had completed his first band arrangement and played his trom-

NAME: Alton Glenn Miller

BORN: March 1, 1904, Clarinda, Iowa

MARRIED: Helen Burger

ACCOMPLISHMENTS: 1937: wrote "Moonlight Serenade"; 1939–1941: Glenn Miller Band was the number one band in the United States; 1942: formed the Glenn Miller Army Air Force Band.

HIT RECORDINGS: "Little Brown Jug," "In the Mood," "Chattanooga Choo Choo," "Tuxedo Junction," "Moonlight Serenade."

QUOTE: "A band ought to have a sound all of its own. It ought to have a personality."

bone with various bands while planning his own band. Although his first band failed, his second succeeded beyond his dreams; and Miller found his "sound." While the clarinet played the melody, both alto and tenor saxophones backed it. The tempo, of course, was "swing."

With this new sound, Miller's popularity rose, and his original compositions and sales records secured his musical reputation. But it was his self-less act of volunteering for the army that established Glenn Miller as a legend.

BEGINNING A NEW CAREER

With the United States embroiled in World War II, Miller tried to enlist but was too old at age thirty-eight. Never one to give up, Miller next wrote to Brigadier General Charles Young of the United States Army and requested an officer's commission that would allow him to lead a modernized band that would "put a little more spring into the feet of our marching men and a little more joy into their hearts."

In 1942, the army still played martial music and marched to the strains of John Philip Sousa, but General Young evidently agreed with Miller that the army's music needed some modernization. The band leader's proposition was too good for the general to pass up, and Alton Glenn Miller was inducted into the army in October 1942.

A LEGEND OF THE AIR FORCE

Although Miller was inducted into the army, he was soon transferred to the air corps, where the Glenn Miller Band was destined to become a part of air force history. In the air corps, Miller raised money for war bonds and had a weekly radio program that helped recruit young men. Glenn himself arranged a transfer to London for his band so they could raise the morale of the troops stationed overseas. In its first year, the Glenn Miller Army Air Force Band performed eight hundred concerts.

Glenn Miller. Photo by Archive Photos.

MOONLIGHT SERENADE

In late 1944, Miller was completing plans for moving the band to Paris for a six-week concert tour. On a snowy December 15, Miller and his pilot took off across the English Channel in a single-engine plane. It was not until the band arrived in Paris three days later that they and the world discovered that Miller's plane had never reached Paris. No debris was found, and the air force pronounced Miller missing and presumed dead.

Glenn Miller's band remained intact and, for the remainder of the war, continued to perform for the troops. Today, the air force still has a Glenn Miller Band, now called the Airmen of Note. Sixty years after the loss of their leader, Miller's legacy still tries to "put a little more spring into the feet of our marching men and a little more joy into their hearts."

THE GLENN MILLER FESTIVAL
CLARINDA, IOWA

D. Fran Morley

Big band music is a true American art form, so I wasn't surprised when I learned that the largest big band music festival in the world takes place every year deep within America's heartland. The little town of Clarinda, in the southwest corner of Iowa, has been recognized as one of the best small towns in America. During one weekend every June, this town is one of the best places for people like me who love big band music—specifically the music of the great Glenn Miller, one of Clarinda's favorite sons.

Miller, who led one of the most loved and respected bands of the late 1930s and early 1940s, stood out from the crowd of popular big bands. He created his own unique swing sound with arrangements that relied on intricate interplay between clarinets, saxophones, and vocals and featured some of the best improvising soloists in the business. America and the world fell in love with what became known as "the Miller sound."

Last year, I joined forty-five hundred other fans for the Glenn Miller Festival in Clarinda, where we nearly doubled the size of the little town. We were there to enjoy all that Clarinda and the festival have to offer, including museum displays, panel discussions, a dance, and even a parade. But mainly we were there to listen to music from nearly a dozen quality amateur and top-notch professional big bands, some re-creating the classic Miller sound, others preferring the style of Benny Goodman, Harry James, Tommy Dorsey, and other big band leaders.

On the afternoon of my arrival, I strolled the wide, shady streets of downtown Clarinda. Making friends with other visitors from as far away as Japan and Germany, I boarded a bus for a tour of town. We stopped at the high school to view a display of memorabilia from the Glenn Miller Archives at the University of Colorado and then went to the Miller Birthplace Home, a tiny frame cottage typical of many Midwestern homes of the early 1900s. Miller's family moved often in his youth, and although many of the items in the home belonged to the family, the tour guide informed us that nothing was original to the time of his birth in 1904.

> *The music of Glenn Miller is timeless; one hundred years from now, bands will still be playing "In the Mood."*

Still, it was fun to see where this legendary performer was born.

According to the guide, the Glenn Miller Birthplace Society has more than seventeen hundred members from forty-seven states and twenty-four foreign countries. I learned that the Glenn Miller Festival began in 1976 as a way for Clarinda to celebrate our country's bicentennial. The local high school band and a few speakers were the only entertainment at the first event, but the idea caught on. The festival grew slowly at first and then at a rapid pace, gaining international attention in the mid-1980s.

A Japanese businessman who was a big Glenn Miller fan arranged for a band from a girls' high school in Tamana, Japan, to play at the festival, and girls from the school have returned every two years since 1996. They stay with Clarinda residents, so the festival is also a cultural exchange program.

The Miller Birthplace Home is one of Clarinda's most popular landmarks. Photo by P. Michael Whye.

Over the past few years, the festival has featured bands from all over the United States, including U.S. military jazz and big bands as well as bands from Canada, Japan, Holland, Austria, and England. The Airmen of Note, the premier jazz ensemble of the U.S. Air Force and a direct descendant of Miller's Army Air Force Band, are always welcomed at the festival.

After hearing concerts at the high school gym and auditorium, I was hungry for more; and I enjoyed the special big band breakfast at the community center. But perhaps the most wonderful performance came on Friday night when almost everyone in town turned out for the free concert on the courthouse square. After spreading a blanket out on the grass, I watched as the square filled with people of all ages. Longtime friends called out to

each other, and laughter rippled through the gathering. Soon the crowd quieted, and everyone's attention focused on the stage. These were serious music fans, of course, who didn't want to miss a moment of the night's performance.

A cool breeze picked up as the sun went down, and the music seemed to float on its current. As the final rays of sun glinted off the top of the town's stately courthouse and the band played Miller's emotional "Moonlight Serenade," I knew that I had discovered something very special. The music of Glenn Miller is universal and timeless; one hundred years from now, bands will still be playing "In the Mood." For me, however, the music will never sound better than it did on this picture-perfect summer night, here where it was born, in America's heartland.

Robin's Return
Mabel Fundingsland

I opened wide my window
To hear the robin sing;
His silvery notes were wafted
On the breath of early spring.

Snowflakes fluttered from above;
The April air was chill.
Yet he sang from the lilac bush
So near my windowsill.

I listened and I pondered;
To him the world belonged,
For the joys of Easter morning
Were echoed in his song.

On the Edge of Spring
Kay Hoffman

I thought I heard a robin sing;
It seemed it could not be,
But then I spied him proudly perched
On bough of leafless tree.

The sky was drear and overcast;
The lacy snowflakes fell.
Upon my winter-weary heart
He cast his magic spell.

He didn't need the sun to shine;
His happy song did ring.
I think the angels must have joyed
To hear that wee bird sing.

With humble heart I listened there
Until he flew away.
He never knew the cheer he brought
To others on that day.

How caring is our loving God
Who sends the bird to sing
When the heart's grown winter-weary
Just on the edge of spring.

Another Spring
Patience Strong

There's a new note in the choirs that sing
    upon the leafless boughs.
There's a new song in the air today,
    a song that seems to rouse
The joy of life, the hopes and dreams
    grown cold in winter hours,
Waking all the old, sweet thoughts
    of blossoms, buds, and flowers.

There's a promise of delight
    in every throb of melody;
There's a stirring and a quickening
    in every bush and tree.
So sing your heart out, little bird!
    Your music seems to bring
The news that God is sending
    to the world another spring.

Top left: An American robin surveys the spring
day. Photo by Scott Hanrahan/ImageState.
Right: A birdhouse offers a view of a spring garden
in Fishcreek, Wisconsin. Photo by Jessie Walker.

Bits
and
Pieces

There's music in the sighing of a reed;
There's music in the gushing of a rill;
There's music in all things, if men had ears:
Their earth is but an echo of the spheres.
—George Gordon Byron

Music resembles poetry; in each
Are nameless graces which no methods teach,
And which a master hand alone can reach.
—Alexander Pope

The music in my heart I bore
Long after it was heard no more.
—William Wordsworth

Music is the language spoken by angels.
—Henry Wadsworth Longfellow

Music hath charms to soothe the savage
breast, to soften rocks, or bend a knotted oak.
—William Congreve

*A*ll one's life is music if one
touches notes rightly and in time.
—*John Ruskin*

*A*ll music is what awakes from you when
you are reminded by the instruments.
—*Walt Whitman*

*T*here is sweet music here that softer falls
Than petals from blown roses on the grass.
—*Alfred, Lord Tennyson*

*I*t is not hard to compose, but it is
wonderfully hard to let the superfluous
notes fall under the table.
—*Johannes Brahms*

EARTH'S EASTER PSALM

Ethel Romig Fuller

Waking from its winter calm,
Earth joins in an Easter psalm;
A psalm in praise of growing things—
Larks, singing, mount on swift, glad wings;
A sudden small swamp fiddle thrums;
On a log, a partridge drums;
A pheasant shrieks his ecstasy;
Bees drone in a petaled tree.

Water's voice is everywhere,
A reverently whispered prayer;
Children's footsteps follow after
The swinging chimes of their young laughter.
Waking from its winter calm,
Earth joins in an Easter psalm.

*Surrounded by a friendly flock, a child admires
an early spring blossom in* DREAMING *by artist
Luigi Chialiva. Image from Galerie George,
London, Great Britain. Fine Art Photographic
Library, London/Art Resource, New York.*

The Jonquils

Ann Haughaboo Chin

I think she knew,
When she planted
Those brown bulbs by the door,
That a hundred years hence
Gold would cover
The yard and the orchard and more.

Long since the house is gone.
Spring plows have turned the sod
And spread this beauty acres wide—
A legacy of jonquils to multiply and nod.

She must have seen them in her dreams,
Spanning the little hill.
Perhaps even now
Through a window of heaven
She leans and smiles as we fill
Our arms with her golden leaven.

Who sows a field, or trains a flower, or plants a tree is more than all.

—JOHN GREENLEAF WHITTIER

Golden jonquils line a weathered fence in Skagit County, Washington. Photo by Terry Donnelly.

Readers' Reflections

Readers are invited to submit original poetry for possible publication in future issues of Ideals. Please send typed copies only; manuscripts will not be returned. Writers receive $10 for each published submission. Send material to Readers' Reflections, Ideals Publications, 535 Metroplex Drive, Suite 250, Nashville, Tennessee 37211.

April Gifts

Elaine B. Porter
Watertown, Massachusetts

Your dawn of sunshine does impart
The warmth of spring upon my heart.
Forsythia sprays its radiant hue
Against your sky of cloudless blue.
Rows of tulips on the lawn
Sparkle as they stretch and yawn.

And as we mark the moving hours,
Clouds roll in with sudden showers.
But not with sky too dark to be
Without some hope for all to see
At the very end of day
The sun peek through to leave its rays.

O April day, you seem to know
How to coax the flowers to grow.
Your sun and moisture in good measure
Give another spring to treasure.

Surprise

Verns Siegrist
Lititz, Pennsylvania

To my surprise this morning when
I flung the shutters wide,
Rain refreshed the wilted world
Across the countryside.

Rain arrived like teardrops
While all were fast asleep.
No one heard the pitter-patter
Or the cleansing of its sweep.

The grass and all the flowers
Were clean and gleaming bright
When I awoke this morning
To greet the morning light.

I love surprises, and this morn
I flung the shutters wide
To find God sent the showers
To kiss our countryside.

Spring Rain

Crystal Fisher
Cedar Rapids, Iowa

The soft song of the falling rain.
The pitter-patter on the windowpane.
The whispering winds woo the trees
By the barely brushing balmy breeze.
The splishing splooshing of puddle's splash—
Galosh-clad children jump and laugh.
Pastel petals play to and fro,
Then wisp and whirl to the world below.
The heady aroma of the healthy earth.
The velvet lawn and dank, dark dirt.
The dandelions dare display their rays,
Bringing faith to the hope of sunny days.
Birds chitter and chirp and chatter and chime
While robins surrender their serenading rhyme.
The little drops utter their last lilting lull.
The Maker holds His breath to this madrigal,
The soft song of the falling rain.
Rejoice in the Lord, it's spring again!

Springtime Walk Through Town

Ruth J. Wahlberg
Two Harbors, Minnesota

Last summer's residue lies strewn around.
A walk through town unmasks a springtime scent
Where autumn refuse piles are evident,
Emitting odors from the thawing ground.
In early spring, no beauty can be found,
No pastel colors as a complement
To naked trees that need spring's nourishment
So barren gardens can be flower crowned.
We need a fresh spring rain to purge the earth,
To make it green and cleanse the stagnant air,
Bring fragrances of Maytime's fragile blooms
Which come, resplendent, after April's birth.
Then beauteous spring would flourish everywhere,
Washed and refreshed with nature's sweet perfumes.

Inviting the Rain

Yvonne Griffeth
Lusk, Wyoming

The crackling earth
With yellow grass and brown dirt
Invites the rain from the sky,
Wanting to change
To its spring color, green,

Holding its breath
For its first drenching drink
Since the last one
With white snow.
Tiny seeds wait under the earth

To sprout a splash of flowers
Where butterflies prance
And ladybugs dance.
Oh, please won't you come,
Spring showers!

A SLICE OF LIFE

REAL SPRING

Edna Jaques

Real spring has come, not shifty, windy rain,
But violets growing down a quiet lane.
Not sudden gusts of cold from off the sea,
But quivering wings in every budding tree.

Real spring with days like jewels set apart,
And all its age-old hunger in your heart,
An aching need for sun against your face,
And all the old sweet freedom of the race.

Real spring with wide brown furrows wet and bare,
A new young greenness showing everywhere,
New lambs and colts in pastures warm and clean,
Old orchard trees and daisies in between.

A mother hen at shining dusk of day
Finds a warm corner up against the hay
And makes of her own body, safe and crude,
A kindly shelter for her tiny brood.

Wide fields of wheat whose petals one by one
Push small green fingers up to find the sun,
Whose roots lie deep below the furrowed plain,
Seeking their substance from the sun and rain.

Real spring, with all the fragrant lovely earth,
Pulsing with gracious life and joy and birth,
A quickening in the hidden heart of things,
Across the starry dark, the beat of wings.

Robert Duncan was born in Utah and began painting at age eleven, when his grandmother gave him his first set of oil paints. During summers spent on his grandparents' Wyoming ranch, he grew to love the rural lifestyle. Today, Robert, his wife, his six children, and a lively assortment of farm animals live in the little town of Midway, Utah.

A young woman gathers the first blossoms of the season in SPRING TAPESTRY *by artist Robert Duncan. Image provided by Robert Duncan Studios.*

THE SEASON OF THE KATY-BERL TREE

Patsy J. Evans

I stand at the window, watching rain drip from the green umbrella of the Katy-Berl tree. It's just an infant, a spindly little thing, pale shadow of the huge willow that stood in that spot a few months ago. It was an old friend, that willow, and I miss it.

More than thirty years have passed since the day five-year-old Rick came tearing into the kitchen, his blue eyes sparkling. "Hey, Mom! Me and Dad planted you a tree!"

"Dad and I planted a tree," I corrected automatically.

"Did not," he protested, shaking his head. "We did. Me and Dad. Come and see!" His grubby little hand tugged at mine, and I followed him into the backyard.

"See?" he said, pointing to a twig stuck in the ground. "I told you we planted a tree."

I smiled at my husband, and he winked. Neither of us believed it would grow.

But it did. It grew until its graceful branches swept the sky. It was by the tree, rather than the calendar, that I marked the seasons. Around the middle of February, long before the arrival of robins or crocuses, it spouted gold against the somber sky, and I was cheered by its insistent whisper, "Spring is coming, spring is coming."

Later, hummingbirds scrapped at the feeders, and summer storms set the branches to swaying like hula dancers. Snow turned it into a lacy Valentine, decorated with the occasional cardinal. And all year, every year, it littered the yard with leaves and twigs. I loved that tree.

Years, as they have a way of doing, slipped by. The little blue-eyed boy became a man with blue-eyed boys of his own, and they climbed into the broad lap of the old tree just as their father had done. The growing flock of grandchildren and I spread blankets in its shade and enjoyed picnics of peanut butter and jelly sandwiches and lemonade. I spent many summer evenings, a book in my lap, watching the changing pattern of light and shadow,

---

If a tree dies, plant another in its place.

—LINNAEUS

---

thinking of the days when my husband and I were young, when our children—and the tree—were growing up.

The old tree was so much more than leaves and bark and roots; it was part of the landscape of my life. But no earthly thing lives forever; and in time, storms and insects, and even the woodpecker who visited regularly, took their toll.

"You'd better have that tree cut down before it falls," my neighbor said.

One side of the massive trunk was hollow, and I knew that, some day, a storm would bring it crashing down. He was right, of course; I should have had it cut down, but I couldn't. I just couldn't. It was almost like having a dear, old pet put to sleep.

November winds blew loudly and fiercely, and the tree *did* fall, not with a crash, but with a soft little "whoosh." Its branches pressed against the window, the bulk of it resting on the roof, as if some gentle hand had placed it there.

The fallen giant was dismembered and hauled away, and my view was forever changed. For weeks I looked out on the emptiness and felt a haunting sadness. I missed my old friend, missed the sound of wind-flung leaves against my window and the freshly washed smell of its leaves after a rain. I missed its great comforting bulk. And yes, I missed the past, the young woman I was, my husband, my children.

Then one particularly gloomy day, thumbing through my Bible, I came across the familiar passage in Ecclesiastes, "There is a time for everything, and a season for every activity under heaven . . . a time to plant and a time to uproot," and I remembered an article I had read some time ago. It described the wonderful order of the natural world; how, when a forest burns, wildflowers and plants of the open fields, no longer denied food and light by the mature forest, begin to appear; how, if undisturbed, the cycle begins anew; how the whole things turns in perfect motion, like a beautiful, mysterious, ever-changing kaleidoscope.

Yes, I realized, it's true. To everything there *is* a season. My season as a young wife, a young mother, the season of the willow tree, had passed. But season follows season, in God's perfect order, each with its own unique beauty and potential for joy. All I had to do was let go of the old and open my eyes and my arms to the new. Still, the barren view from my window saddened me.

Christmas came. My mother-in-law Kate, who had been ill and unable to shop, and my father, Berl, who never knew what to give a daughter who had long ago outgrown dolls and roller skates, each gave me gifts of cash. When I opened their envelopes, what I saw was not the green of hard-earned dollars, but visions of delicate pink clouds against a blue, blue sky—weeping cherry trees in bloom. I had wanted one for years and now, come spring, something new would grow in that great empty space in the backyard—a Katy-Berl tree.

The rain has stopped, and a gentle breeze ruffles the leaves of the weeping cherry. It was planted in late April, and bore only a few of the pink blooms I cherished. To be honest, it looks pretty pathetic, skinny and gangly, like a teen-ager who hasn't quite figured out what to do with all those arms and legs. But like the willow, it will grow. As I watch, a hummingbird rests there, fragile limbs on fragile limbs, and the perfection of bird and tree takes my breath away.

And so begins another season.

Someday, as we sit in its shade, my grandchildren, perhaps even great-grandchildren, will ask me how the Katy-Berl tree came to be, and I'll tell them stories of Grandma Kate and Grandpa Berl; about the great willow that was just a twig, and all the wonderful things that happened while it grew; how its season passed and something new and beautiful was planted in its place. Together we'll marvel at the pink fountain spouting into the springtime sky, or watch snow lace its branches. And I'll tell them how everything has its own season, and, like a river with many bends, one flows into another in perfect order, in the most remarkable way.

A weeping cherry tree blooms in Seattle's Washington Park Arboretum.
Photo by Terry Donnelly.

Spring Fever

S. Omar Barker

If it's big, so much the better;
If it's small I'll love it still,
Just so long as I can putter
With a bit of soil to till.

It's my pathway back to nature
In a restless modern day.
Surely digging in a garden
Beats all other games men play.

Our own green things for the table!
Our own flowers—aren't they nice?
My own patch of God's creation,
My own bit of paradise.

Don't pretend to understand it;
All I know is this one thing:
Life seems incomplete and wasteful
Without gardening in spring.

Being happy is dirt under your fingernails, wearing old clothes, having a good idea get better the longer you work at it, starting a new bed, giving plants away, and listening to rain. —*Geoffrey B. Charlesworth*

Heritage roses cling to an arbor in Multnomah County, Oregon. Photo by Steve Terrill.

Unfoldment
Elizabeth Humerickhouse

Lovely as the turquoise eggs,
Small ovals in a robin's nest,
Young bills will know to break the shell
That hides a robin's roseate breast.
So dormant bulbs beneath the ground,
Concealed by winter's labyrinth,
Know to spear resilient soil
For bloom of purple hyacinth.

As dark brown bulb and turquoise egg
Know to burst for bird and flower,
Love knew to roll away a stone
That sealed the Resurrection hour.

Easter Legacy
L. Mildred Harris

From Easter Eve to Easter Day
Was just a little time away,
But something happened in those hours
That gave the world triumphant powers.

Now Easter brings to us each year
The strength to triumph over fear;
And where we've found a stone before,
We, too, may find an open door.

*Our Lord has written the promise of
the Resurrection not in books alone,
but in every leaf in springtime.*
—MARTIN LUTHER

Turquoise ovals brighten a nest in APPLE
BLOSSOM AND A BIRD'S NEST *by artist H. Barnard
Grey. Image from Burlington Paintings,
London, Great Britain. Fine Art Photographic
Library, London/Art Resource, New York.* 85

Readers' Forum

Snapshots from Our Ideals Readers

Left: Ryan Frangoul takes advantage of a fine spring day to tiptoe through the tulips as gently as a two-year-old is able. He is the grandson of Edna and Garnes Reed of Pratt, West Virginia.

Bottom left: During a garden visit, sixteen-month-old Robert Christian Edwards discovers that these tulips are indeed real. The photo was sent to us by Robert Christian's great-grandmother, Virginia Jones of Blairs, Virginia.

Bottom right: Kayla Jean Baez has dirt on her cute face from helping her great-grandmother, Eva Jean Butcavage, weed her flower garden. Eva Jean, of Wernersville, Pennsylvania, tells us that Kayla is a pretty good little helper, especially for being only one and a half.

Top left: Katherine M. Schwabauer of Salem, Oregon, tells us that she is delighted when little Kailey Nicole Campbell, who lives next door, comes to visit her "Grandma Katherine." In this snapshot, Kailey Nicole stops to really smell the flowers during one of her visits.

Top right: There is no happier place than Grandma's flower garden in spring, at least to tiny Niccole Bergland. She is the granddaughter of Don and Sandy Malenfant of Colorado Springs, Colorado.

Bottom right: Devin Baber didn't realize that this little garden bench was meant for decor only. His grandmother, June Baber, of Newmarket, Ontario, Canada, tells us that Devin thought the bench was his special garden seat and enjoyed it each time he was in the yard.

THANK YOU
Edna and Garnes Reed, Virginia Jones, Eva Jean Butcavage, Katherine M. Schwabauer, Don and Sandy Malenfant, June Baber, and Marion and Bernice Wade for sharing your family photographs with *Ideals*. We hope to hear from other readers who would like to share snapshots with the *Ideals* family. Please include a self-addressed, stamped envelope if you would like the photos returned. Keep your original photographs for safekeeping and send duplicate photos along with your name, address, and telephone number to:

Readers' Forum
Ideals Publications
535 Metroplex Drive, Suite 250
Nashville, Tennessee 37211

Below: Six-month-old Elizabeth Diane Wade wears a yellow dress to match the spring flowers she is discovering in her Aunt Brenda's daffodil patch. The snapshot was sent to us by Elizabeth's grandparents, Marion and Bernice Wade of Hillsville, Virginia.

Publisher, Patricia A. Pingry
Editor, Michelle Prater Burke
Managing Editor, Peggy Schaefer
Designer, Marisa Calvin
Production Manager, Travis Rader
Copy Editor, Melinda Rathjen
Editorial Assistant, Patsy Jay
Contributing Editors, Lansing Christman, Pamela Kennedy, and Lisa Ragan

ACKNOWLEDGMENTS

ANDERSON, BEVERLY J. "Easter Bouquet." Used by permission of Daisy Kerr. BARKER, S. OMAR. "Spring Fever." Used by permission of Marjorie A. Phillips. CALVERT, CATHERINE. "The Egg Hunt" from *Victoria*, April 2000. Used by permission of *Victoria* magazine. FIELD, RUTH B. "Young Spring." Used by permission of Natalie Field Bevis. FUNDINGSLAND, MABEL. "Robin's Return." Used by permission of Marlene Hanson. GIOVANNI, NIKKI. "Springtime" from *Spin a Soft Black Song* by Nikki Giovanni. Copyright © 1971, 1985 by the author. Reprinted by permission of Hill and Wang, a division of Farrar, Straus and Giroux, LLC. JAQUES, EDNA. "Real Spring" from *Beside Still Waters* by Edna Jaques. Published in Canada by Thomas Allen & Son Limited, 1952. Used by permission of the publisher. LINTON, MARY E. "April Promise." Used by permission of Richard W. Kobelt. STOFFEL, BETTY W. "White-Petaled Laughter." Used by permission of E. Lee Stoffel. STRONG, PATIENCE. "Another Spring" from *Food for Thought*. April 14, 1949. Used by permission of Rupert Crew Limited, London. THOMAS, ESTHER KEM. "Buds and Bonnets." Used by permission of Frederick A. Thomas. Our sincere thanks to the following authors and heirs whom we were unable to locate: The estate of Ethel Romig Fuller for "Earth's Easter Psalm"; the estate of L. Mildred Harris for "Easter Legacy"; Daniel Whitehead Hicky for "The Secret" from *Never the Nightingale*, copyright © 1951 by Daniel Whitehead Hicky; the estate of Edgar Daniel Kramer for "Wasted Hours"; and the estate of Evelyn Gates Shisler for an excerpt from "Arbutus."

STATEMENT OF OWNERSHIP, MANAGEMENT AND CIRCULATION (REQUIRED BY FORM 3526)

1. Publication Title: Ideals. 2. Publication Number: 0019-137X. 3. Filing Date: August 16, 2002. 4. Issue Frequency: 6. 5. Number of Issues Published Annually: 6. 6. Annual Subscription Price: $19.95. 7. Office of publication: Guideposts, A Church Corporation, 39 Seminary Hill Road, Carmel, NY 10512. 8. Location of headquarters: Guideposts, A Church Corporation, 39 Seminary Hill Road, Carmel, NY 10512. 9. The names and addresses of the publisher and the editor-in-chief are: Patricia A. Pingry, Ideals Publications, A Division of Guideposts, 535 Metroplex Dr., Ste. 250, Nashville, TN 37211; Editor: Michelle Prater Burke (same as publisher); Managing Editor: Michelle Prater Burke (same as publisher). 10. Owner: Guideposts, A Church Corporation, a New York not for-profit corporation, 39 Seminary Hill Road, Carmel, NY 10512. Names and addresses of individual owners; None. 11. The known bondholders, mortgagees, and other security holders owning or holding one percent or more of total amount of bonds, mortgages or other securities: None. 12. The exempt status has not changed during preceding 12 months. 13. Publication Name: Ideals. 14. Issue Date for Circulation Data: Thanksgiving '01 thru Friendship '02. 15. Average number of copies each issue during preceding twelve months: a. total number of copies printed: 207,813; b. (1) paid and/or requested circulation through outside-county mail subscriptions: 145,719; (2) paid and/or requested circulation through in-county subscriptions: None; (3) paid and/or requested circulation through dealer sales: 8,198; (4) paid and/or requested circulation through other classes: None; c. total paid and/or requested circulation: 153,916. d. (1) free distribution by mail through outside-county: 1,982; (2) free distribution by mail through in-county: None; (3) free distribution by mail through other classes: None; e. free distribution outside the mail: None; f. total free distribution: 9,193; g. total distribution: 163,109; h. copies not distributed: 44,704; i. total: 207,813. Percent Paid and/or requested circulation: 94.4%. Actual number of copies of single issue published nearest to filing date: 15.a. total number of copies printed: 147,171; b. (1) paid and/or requested circulation through outside-county mail subscriptions: 126,652; (2) paid and/or requested circulation through in-county subscriptions: None; (3) paid and/or requested circulation through dealer sales: 1,281; (4) paid and/or requested circulation through other classes: None; c. total paid and/or requested circulation: 127,933; d. (1) free distribution by mail through outside-county: 1,000; (2) free distribution by mail through in-county: None; (3) free distribution by mail through other classes: None; e. free distribution outside the mail: None; f. total free distribution: 1,000; g. total distribution: 128,933; h. copies not distributed: 18,238; i. total: 147,171. Percent Paid and/or requested circulation: 99.2%. 16. This Statement of Ownership will be printed in the Easter '03 issue of this publication. 17. I certify that the statements made to me above are correct and complete. Signed John F. Temple, President

Who is the Jesus
about whom we sing?

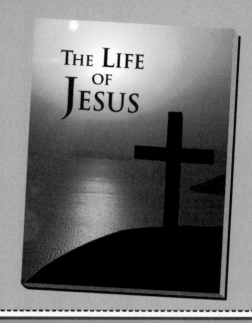

Jesus Christ healed the sick, preached to the multitudes, and calmed the raging seas. But to us today, Jesus is our friend, companion, comforter, and savior. The Gospels give us the facts about His life here on earth. But to gain a more complete and personal picture of the Christ, we must go to written stories and poems by His followers. For Jesus is most alive when He is embraced in the hearts of believers.

Gathered together in an exquisitely beautiful book entitled *THE LIFE OF JESUS* are these extensive writings, each of which contribute a unique look at Jesus. This lavishly illustrated, over-sized book first explores the life of Jesus through the Scriptures, and then through the writings of Christian poets and storytellers—both ancient and contemporary. Each writer brings his or her own personal glimpse of our Lord, and the portrait of Jesus that emerges is of a tender, loving, and *living* Savior.

You'll be inspired and encouraged by this huge collection of Scripture, poems, essays, and stories. And when you finish reading these selections and close the cover of *THE LIFE OF JESUS*, you'll find that the real Jesus, the historical Savior, has walked into your heart.

Return the Free Examination Certificate today to preview *THE LIFE OF JESUS* for 30 days FREE . . . and receive FREE *THE WORDS OF THE LORD* booklet just for ordering.

COMPLETE THE FREE EXAMINATION CERTIFICATE AND MAIL TODAY FOR YOUR 30-DAY PREVIEW.

No need to send money now!

BRIGHTEN SOMEONE'S DAY WITH FAITH. . .SHARE THE JOY OF
GUIDEPOSTS WISHING WELL GREETINGS!

Less Than 99¢ a card!

Do you know someone whose spirits need lifting? A family member recovering from an illness, or a special friend who needs to know you're thinking of them? Show you care with *Guideposts Wishing Well Greetings*—a lovely new collection of faith-graced cards that will banish their blues and wrap them in an embrace of caring.

Birthdays, weddings, holidays, anniversaries...there seems to be a card for just about everything these days. But what about a card that celebrates something more precious, a card that lets someone know just how important they are in your life?

Guideposts Wishing Well Greetings is filled with cards just like these—cards that celebrate the simple joy of compassion and caring and spread the message of God's love at the same time.

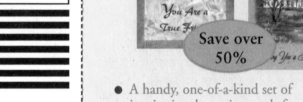

Save over 50%

- A handy, one-of-a-kind set of inspirational greeting cards from Guideposts.

- 15 beautifully illustrated 4 5/8" x 6 7/8" cards—each with messages of healing and greetings of prayer.

- Designed for loved ones of all ages.

- Exclusively from Guideposts—not available in any store!

- An amazing value—less than 99¢ a card!

Each card in this unique collection features an inspiring message, uplifting Scripture, and a gorgeous watercolor illustration. Best of all, there's an uplifting Guideposts story or poem on the back of each one! Save over 50% off the average store-bought brands! And with 15 different cards to choose from, you'll always have the perfect card to express your feelings.

Cheer up someone you care deeply about. Spread the blessings of God's love. Say "YES" to *Guideposts Wishing Well Greetings* and show someone special you're thinking of them!

FREE EXAMINATION CERTIFICATE

YES! Please rush me the one-of-a-kind set of *Guideposts Wishing Well Greetings* at no risk or obligation. I understand that I may examine all 15 cards FREE for 30 days. If I decide to keep them, I will be billed later at the low Guideposts price of only $12.95, plus postage and handling. That's more than 50% off the average retail price! If I am not completely satisfied, I will return them to you within 30 days and owe nothing.

Total sets ordered: _____

Please print your name and address:

_____
NAME

_____
ADDRESS

_____
CITY   STATE   ZIP

❏ Please Bill Me ❏ Charge My: ❏ MasterCard ❏ Visa

Credit Card #:

☐☐☐☐ ☐☐☐☐ ☐☐☐☐ ☐☐☐☐

Expiration Date: _____

Signature _____

Allow 4 weeks for delivery. Orders subject to credit approval.
Send no money now. We will bill you later.
www.guidepostsbooks.com

Printed in USA
011/202024030

NO NEED TO SEND MONEY NOW!